Paths of the Shepherd

Brian Troxel

ACKNOWLEDGMENTS

I wish to express my love and gratitude to my wife of 38 years, Linda. She has faithfully stood with me and painstakingly endeavored to edit my attempts to put thoughts on paper!

It is also with much appreciation I acknowledge Dr. C.R. Oliver and Betty Oliver who spent much time and effort to transform this collection of writings into a finished book.

FOREWORD

Those who seek insight into the multiple facets of this popular Psalm will find it here in Brian Troxel's unique treatment. His blending of word studies, wisdom from past authorities and his own life experiences move the text in a rapid manner.

Troxel treats the Psalm as an expression of his own heart, while emphasizing the universality of David's masterpiece. He uses quotes from many sources to break the sequences into chapters, all the while inserting quotable insights of his own. Three such instances offer a view into the character of the book.

"The secret of the message of the valley is that we walk through it. We do not succumb to it; we do not spend our life sitting in it; we walk THROUGH IT. We keep moving, trusting, and walking until the DAY dawns and HIS GLORY is seen! These valleys are not crossed over because of the absence of fear; they are crossed over in spite of the fear!" Devotional 11

"God's Word to HIS PEOPLE today is one of grave importance, one that reveals and lays bare the reason that we are in such disarray, impotence and apathy." Devotional 16

"Power without character is the great evil in the world today, whether it be political, financial, judicial, or above all, religious." Devotional 22

Brian's comments range from words of encouragement to those of rebuke as the mystery of Psalm 23 unfolds in his hands. His moral character and humility show up throughout his writing and are rare ingredients in today's marketplace.

Dr. C. R. Oliver, PhD, OEA Intl
Zadok Publications, The Woodlands, Texas

Table of Contents

Introduction

"For the Son of man is come to seek and to save that which was lost."

LUKE 19:10

The relationship of the Shepherd has been a very real one for me. I had the personal experience of Him seeking me out when He, in His great love, came unbidden into my room some 42 years ago and transformed a lost and hopeless man. I have known the discipline of his rod and the guidance of His staff and have indeed found comfort in both. Always His love has kept me in His grasp and I carry an unspeakable debt of gratitude to the Chief Shepherd of my soul.

This collection of brief devotions is meant to serve as seeds sown into the hearts and minds of those who love and follow the Great Shepherd. They are not intended to be exhaustive teachings in themselves but merely gateways into His pasture. This small book is offered with the prayer that the

1

Holy Spirit would be pleased to encourage others to find His paths which will lead to still waters and the restoration of their souls.

PSALM 23

Devotional One

"The Lord is my shepherd..."

PSALM 23:1

"The Lord is my shepherd" is more than just poetry, more than a nice theological concept and much more than simply a feel good religious verse. To those who know Him, it is the sum total of the fundamental and essential aspect of our relationship with Him. The Hebrew name for **Lord** here is **YHWH**. It is the Name of God revealed to the man Moses as he was being sent back into Egypt as deliverer of His people. It is a name that depicted Glory and Majesty to such an extent that traditionally it was not even spoken out of great reverence and respect. Yet here that great name is being divinely connected to that of a Shepherd! This is the same great name that carries with it the meaning of One of endless, eternal self-existence, clothed in omnipotence and infinite majesty, by whose power all of Egypt was destroyed on such a scale and in such a manner that to this day, it remains unsurpassed in the revelation of the Judgments of God. Let us ponder the significance of the connection of such a God to that of not only a Shepherd, but a personal Shepherd who cares for the life of His own.

To know, in some religious way, that the Lord is as **a** shepherd will convey little in terms of the power and comfort of the relationship in knowing He is the director of our steps. In this statement, we see this Great and Holy God is not only **a** shepherd but it is essential for us to know experientially that He is **my** shepherd! This foundational truth can only be true if there is, within the core of my being, a new birth experience that has translated me from the rebellious nature of a goat to that of a lamb desirous to be submissive and taught in the Way of our God. Only by us becoming sheep in nature will we fully appreciate the wisdom and care of our great shepherd.

The Lord is my Shepherd! Let the truth of this sink deep into our consciousness. Let the power of all it means convey a warmth and comfort to our troubled hearts in times of distress. Let it assure us we are not mere wandering souls left to our own resources. Let it communicate to us a sense of purpose, a special relationship with the Almighty God who has taken upon **Himself** the responsibility to lead us through the dangers of this life.

THE LORD ALONE IS MY SHEPHERD

The Lord is my Shepherd! We hear many today say that some religious leader is their Pastor or Shepherd; it must grieve the heart of God for such things to even be considered! HE is my Shepherd. There is no man who can chart the dark waters of my needs, no man who can be made unto me wisdom and strength, and no other who can keep me in the way of righteousness and truth. HE ALONE IS MY SHEPHERD (Isaiah 40:11). He alone is your shepherd. You will never read anywhere in the scriptures of a man being **my** apostle, **my** teacher or **my** prophet. He has given the church ministries of the Apostolic, Prophetic, Evangelistic, Shepherding and Teaching expressions for the building up of THE Body of Christ. They are simply precious expressions given to help us develop our own personal relationship with our Lord Jesus Christ. There is only ONE SHEPHERD and His name is Jesus. It is the solemn obligation of every true and valid ministry to bring you and me to the place of seeking, knowing, and living our lives in Him.

> "I am the good shepherd. The good shepherd gives His life for the sheep."

JOHN 10:11

SELAH.

PSALM 23

Devotional Two

"The Lord is my shepherd..." Part 2

PSALM 23:1

"The Lord is my shepherd." We have no indication from the scriptures when, in David's life, he wrote this beautiful Psalm. Whether it was at a time as a young shepherd boy out alone tending the sheep of his father, whether in a cave running from King Saul or as the King of Israel, we only know the power of this statement was true in all of the circumstances in which David found himself. One of the most powerful words in this simple statement is the word "is." This word conveys the truth to us of **YHWH,** the Eternal One, in the most wondrous terms—**present tense**. Though truth is eternal, it does not afford us much in terms of value and meaning unless it is present tense, in the here and now. "The Lord **is** my shepherd." This is the glory of faith, for faith ever seeks to impart to us the present truth of God's being and the comfort and power of all that He is in our present circumstances.

Religion has a way of acknowledging God in the past. Martha met Jesus *after* Lazarus had died; "Lord, if thou hadst been here, my brother had not died." In other words, the present circumstances would have been different if God had responded sooner; the present situation could have been prevented. Many of God's people have become bitter and despondent with this outlook. They are not able to reconcile the place in which they find themselves with the tender loving care of the Lord our Shepherd. Faith is to bring the truth that His tender loving care **is** with us in the moments of great distress and sorrow. "The Lord **IS** my Shepherd!" Martha's expression of disappointment was the outcome of a faith that had not yet developed into the "now" of life.

Religion also has a way of meeting the present situation with a futuristic outlook. Unable to grasp the reality of the now, Martha then responds to Jesus' statement of, "Thy brother shall rise again," with a quick reference to a future event; "I know that he shall rise again in the resurrection at the last day." Both of these responses contain traces of faith but fall short of THE FAITH.

Faith is the element of our relationship with our great Shepherd that is a living thing. Jesus' parable of the mustard seed reveals a living thing that grows and develops over time. The past and the present responses of Martha take into account the power and the truth of who Christ is, yet His desire for us is to see Him as the great I AM. The now faith is what makes men and women of God strong and unshakeable in the world in which we live.

> "God *is* our refuge and strength, A
> very present help in trouble"

> PSALM 46:1-2

It is in our journey with Him that the power of this truth begins to enter into the core of our hearts; our Shepherd is a present help. The situation we **now** face we face with the knowledge that He is, right at this moment, our Shepherd, our refuge, our strength and a **present** help in trouble.

We read in Psalm 3 of a time when David was on the run from his own son and the people of Israel did not come to David's aid.

> "Lord, how they have increased who
> trouble me! Many *are* they who rise

up against me. Many *are* they who say of me, "*There is* no help for him in God." *Selah"*

PSALM 3:1-2

He was on the run with a small band of faithful ones, and the voices of the multitudes around him in his day were saying, "There is no help for him in God." Have we not heard such voices within our own hearts as we look at the circumstances before us? Have our hearts not sunk at the enormity and the hopelessness of the thing we were facing? Let us be encouraged in our God, for David responded to that dark hour with:

> "But You, O Lord, *are* a shield for me, My glory and the One who lifts up my head. I cried to the Lord with my voice, And He heard me from His holy hill. *Selah* I lay down and slept; I awoke, for the Lord sustained me. I will not be afraid of ten thousands of people Who have set *themselves* against me all around"

PSALM 3:3-6

These declarations of faith in the midst of dark and trying times can only come from those who, in following their great Shepherd, have grown into the place of knowing:

"The Lord IS my Shepherd!

"Blessed be the Name of the Lord!

SELAH.

PSALM 23

Devotional Three

"I shall not want…"

PSALM 23:1

"Want," for most of us, is not a concept with which we are familiar. We live in a land blessed with abundance. While in other parts of the world there is great want and need for the necessities of life, we here see a great want for the excesses of life. When we truly believe the Lord is our Shepherd and that He provides our needs, we should be free from the lust of things externally and internally. We should be finding rest in His provisions and His great providence. Many of us work day and night to pay for the excesses, not the necessities. "We have to make a living" is our reasoning when, in reality, we have sold ourselves into a life of servitude for the "things" this world has to offer. We are not talking here of some religious vow of poverty. We are speaking of a contentment in the Lord our Shepherd, a freedom from the passion for "things" that would entice and burden us with a life of debt to this world. Our lifestyle should not enslave us but rather free us to serve our God.

I SHALL NOT WANT is a life that is free to follow and serve our Great Shepherd. **I SHALL NOT WANT** is a life that is free from the lusts, passions and entanglements of this world. **I SHALL NOT WANT** is a life that has found peace in knowing HE is our provider, that HE really is all we need. It is a freedom from the pressure of this world to have and hold more. For in truth, those things can have a hold on us. WE ARE ALWAYS THE SERVANT OF THAT WHICH OUR HEART DESIRES. That is why Jesus says:

> "Take heed and beware of covetousness, for one's life does not consist in the abundance of the things he possesses"

LUKE 12:15

Covetousness is a condition of the heart. It steals the affections of our heart with great subtlety, slowly causing our focus to change. The reason we do something is altered from that which is good and

14

necessary to that which satisfies a lust or a desire. A contented life in this world is the result of seeking, desiring and living within the provision and way of the Lord our Shepherd. As we, in the spirit of thankfulness and praise, make our requests known unto Him, we begin to discover His peace in our lives. It is a battle to keep our eyes focused on the **One** who is our provision and our God. We are reminded in John's Gospel:

> "Love not the world, neither the things that are in the world. If any man love the world, the love of the Father is not in him. For all that is in the world, the lust of the flesh, and the lust of the eyes, and the pride of life, is not of the Father, but is of the world. And the world passeth away, and the lust thereof: but he that doeth the will of God abideth for ever"

I JOHN 2:15

I SHALL NOT WANT is the fruit of a life that is finding its contentment in the Life amd provision of THE LORD OUR SHEPHERD. May we daily seek this life of simplicity and rest. <u>To abide in the Love OF the Father is to be free from the love of the World</u>. This freedom is found as we displace one

15

love with a greater Love. We are reminded by the Apostle Paul in Colossians to, **"Set your affection on things above, not on things on the earth."**

"THE LORD IS MY SHEPHERD; I SHALL NOT WANT"

SELAH.

PSALM 23

Devotional Four

"I shall not want…" Part 2

PSALM 23:1

The Hebrew word used here for want not only implies a wanting of things, but it can also imply a lack of something. It can speak of being destitute and wanting. God's people, who walk in God's ways, will never lack the supply of His Grace to accomplish His Will. This is a place that requires much growth and development as we follow our Shepherd. Within the processes of our Heavenly Father, we encounter circumstances and situations within and without that are clearly beyond our resources to meet. We are faced with our own poverty and lack of development to meet the situation. We find ourselves looking outside to a God who is in the heavens. We see ourselves here and Him there, and we feel the poverty and discouragement that comes from such an arrangement. However, in the passing of time, we begin to discover that though our Father is in Heaven, His SON dwells within us! The hidden resources of His Life begin to open to us as a treasure beckoning us to live and walk in it! How good are His ways and past finding out. For this life that we long for, this peace that passes all understanding, is not to be found anywhere else but in Christ. It is for this reason we do not despair of the way, for that Living Christ (if we have been born of Him) dwells in our very hearts by faith. He is no longer afar off; He is near to us, even in our hearts. For the wonder of the New Covenant is, "Christ **in** you the hope of Glory". This life of discovery is the privilege we all have as His children.

Paul, in his own experience, spoke of this transition of moving into the depths of God's economy.

> "Not that I speak in respect of want: for I have learned, in whatsoever state I am, therewith to be content. I know both how to be abased, and I know how to abound: everywhere and in all things I am instructed both to be full and to be hungry, both to

abound and to suffer need. I can do
all things through Christ which
strengtheneth me."

PHILLIPIANS 4:11-13

This place of contentment is a grace learned in the face of various trials and temptations. We need not despair of the height to which one must seemingly attain to know of this life. For it is in following hard after our Shepherd that this life of victory and strength is found. Paul was an avid learner; he was ever looking and discovering the riches of the Glory of God in Christ Jesus. May we be encouraged in all of the circumstances of life to take our eyes off the trial and turn our eyes upon Jesus, the source and supply of all we need! May we, as Peter, see Jesus walking upon the waters of the storm and feel the wonder of the impulse of faith to walk as HE walks. The glory that HE desires to bring us into is part of our inheritance in Him.

The transition of life within us requires much testing and trial. These things are not to be learned in a classroom; they must become ours through the medium of walking with Him. God's purpose is to reveal a people who stand in the midst of the storms, those who reign in Life by Jesus Christ, those who glory in tribulations and persecutions.

Though we feel we fall short of these things, nevertheless, as we walk with Him, the hidden resources of the Christ within will become the source of our strength. The full purpose of the New Covenant is to bring us to the place where what is true in Him, will be True in us (1 John 4:17). Let us not despair for "faithful is He that has called us," and He who has called us will complete that which He has begun!

"THE LORD IS MY SHEPHERD; I SHALL NOT WANT"

SELAH.

PSALM 23

Devotional Five

"He <u>maketh</u> me to lie down in green pastures..."

PSALM 23:2

Rest is a state of heart that is not dependent upon location or circumstance. Here we see the great "mover" of men causing us to lie down in the rich provisions of His care. How little we realize that some of the great curses of sin are restlessness, anxiety and worry. It is in following the Great Shepherd of our souls that we find a grace ever moving us to places of rest and repose in the assurance that He cares and watches over us. "He maketh" (causes us) to lie down, and so we find that peace that passes understanding. This is a peace that is not as the world gives, dependent upon circumstances, but a peace that is found in HIM as we follow wherever HE leads. Rest and peace are the result of a relationship with the Great Shepherd.

"Take my yoke upon you, and learn of me; for I am meek and lowly in heart: and ye shall find rest unto your souls."

MATTHEW 11:29

It is in being yoked with Him that we learn of Him. Bible schools, teachings, meetings and other activities alone will never cause us to **know** Him . It is in learning of Him we discover that meekness and humility are the conditions of a heart that finds rest and repose in His infinite life. Let us not be discouraged in the way, for we read here that He **maketh** us to lie down. He is ever with us to search out and lead us to discover that peace and rest in Him, rather than in other things.

> "the ark of the covenant of the LORD went before them in the three days' journey, **to search out a resting place for them.**"

NUMBERS 10:33

When we insist on our own way, our own righteousness and our own provisions, we forfeit the very rest we so desperately crave. This rest is reserved for those who are able to submit to the wisdom and way of our Shepherd. We read in the New Covenant of One who is come to shine forth as the Child of the MOST HIGH GOD for this purpose:

"To give light to them that sit in darkness and in the shadow of death, to guide our feet into the way of peace"

LUKE 1:79

How we need to see that rest is the fruit of being in the Way, of allowing Him to guide our feet into the way of Peace. May the Lord stir us anew to be found ever in His Way, to be where He leads and guides us to the green pastures of His provision.

"THE LORD IS MY SHEPHERD...He maketh me to lie down in green pastures"

SELAH.

23

PSALM 23

Devotional Six

QUIET WATERS

"He leadeth me beside the still waters…"

PSALM 23:2

Here again is seen the relationship between the Shepherd and His sheep; it is one of leading and being lead. We are also reminded that the heart of the One who leads us is motivated in bringing us to places of rest and peace. We read in the New Testament that one of the results of the Great Day of Judgment is that God Himself will separate between the sheep and the goats. Many will say, "Lord, Lord" in that day, but it is in the crucible of daily life, in our following Him wherever He goes, that we reveal whether we are, in truth, sheep. Goats do not follow; they insist on their own way and have no inherent ability to follow because that is their nature. **Nature determines relationship--not**

teaching.

In this particular Psalm, we see Him leading us beside still waters (or in the actual Hebrew "Waters of Stillness"). He is ever at work in our lives to bring stillness to the waters of our heart that, in all circumstances, we may be found resting in HIS Love for us. It is here in the still waters we are able to see His Face most clearly, for quiet waters reflect the heavens with a beauty and preciseness that troubled waters will never be able to convey.

> "As in water face answereth to face,
> so the heart of man to man."

PROVERBS 27:19

It is when we are quiet and at rest that He most clearly reveals His heart and purpose to us. We read of the men and women, throughout the Old and New Testament, who knew Him as their Rock, their high tower, their refuge and resting place, and they revealed a quality of character that can only come from relationship and trust. Troubled and bitter waters can only minister strife, anger and resentment because what a person is will be revealed in the waters that flow from his or her heart.

"Out of the same mouth proceedeth blessing and cursing. My brethren, these things ought not so to be. Doth a fountain send forth at the same place sweet water and bitter?"

JAMES 3:11

This is a penetrating question we need to consider in reference to the words of our own heart. If we are being lead of Him, over time the waters that flow from our hearts will be filled with the depth of His wisdom because we are at rest in God. A man at rest with God reveals His way, His truth and His life at all times. It is to such an end that we pray He would continually lead us, that we would faithfully follow and that He would receive all the glory and praise; for His goodness and mercy endures forever. AMEN.

"See in the meantime that your faith brings forth obedience, and God in due time will cause it to bring forth peace."

John Owen

SELAH.

PSALM 23

Devotional Seven

"He restoreth my soul..."

PSALM 23:3

In this journey of life, we slowly begin to realize that we, at our very center and core. need change and transformation. The more we walk with Him, the more we learn of Him. We see the eternal power of God expressed in a love that, in itself, is far beyond our grasp, our understanding and comprehension. The very quality of that love causes us to shy away from Him (who **is** that Love) because of its immensity and power. Yet within our hearts there is a cry and an intense desire to **know** this One, to walk and live within the grip of His Life and to **grow** in the wonder of a deep relationship with Him. It is in this desire to know Him that we discover the Way in which we are to walk so this relationship may become deeper, fuller and more meaningful in our life.

Change is the evidence of a life moving in God. No

one who is active in their pursuit and desire for God can remain unchanged. A religious man may speak right things, may do good works, and may appear spiritual, but if there is not an ongoing work of transformation within his life, there is *an issue* at heart.

The Hebrew Word here for "restore" (and its related forms) is translated 1,339 times in the Old Testament and, with few exceptions, speaks of turning, repentance and change. There are countless times in our walk with Him that we have strayed, wandered or insisted on our own way, yet He mercifully comes and turns us and **restores** us back to the paths of righteousness and truth. He is ever seeking, ever desiring for us to grow and develop in our life with Him. The power of the New Covenant is that we are to "**become** sons of God" (John 1:12). The only way to truly know this life of **"becoming"** is to recognize and embrace the life of change that is necessary for this reality.

Over the years I have come to realize that, of all of God's great gifts and dealings in my life, the gift of repentance is a most prized one. For it is in the things we cling to, obstinately, and sometimes unknowingly, that we experience the bitter pangs of misery and weariness. The relief comes in letting go. The joy comes in turning from ourselves. The peace comes in submitting to His will and His way. "**He** restores our soul;" **He** brings us back to the good and right way. **He** returns us to the green meadows of **His** provisions and the still waters where we find "rest unto our souls" and communion with the One who Loves us.

> "Or despisest thou the riches of His goodness and forbearance and longsuffering: not knowing that **the goodness of God leadeth thee to repentance**."

ROMANS 2:4

How blessed we are to have such a One who suffers long with great patience with each of us, ever seeking to restore us and work within us a heart and a life that is at home with Him.

> "THE LORD IS MY SHEPHERD;
> He restoreth my soul"

SELAH.

PSALM 23

Devotional Eight

"He restoreth my soul…"

PSALM 23:3

What a revelation of our Shepherd's heart! "He restoreth my soul…" is the simple statement that there is no other hope for us; no other means by which our soul can be set free, restored and turned away from its own misery and desolation. "He restoreth my soul…" is the hope and anchor of all those who follow after the Great Shepherd of our souls. It is in Him we have reason to hope; this One so full of Love. Let us realize this Love is not just for us. It is what motivated God to send His only begotten Son into this dark world that "whosoever" believes in Him should not perish but have eternal life (John 3:16). Jesus said, in the introduction of the parable of the Good Shepherd, that He came "… to save that which was lost" (Matthew 18:11). With this in mind, let us realize that what He is to us we are to be to one another.

> "A new commandment I give unto you, that ye love one another; as I have loved you…"

JOHN 13:34

We are to love one another **as** He has loved us. That Shepherd's Heart in Him is to be revealed and worked out in our lives in loving and caring for one another. Truth is not truth until it is **expressed** in the common course of everyday life. If He has so wonderfully expressed His love to us by the unmerited grace of God, should not that same expression flow from our hearts to one another?

> "Brethren, if a man be overtaken in a fault, <u>ye which are spiritual,</u> RESTORE such an one in the spirit of meekness; considering thyself, lest thou also be tempted."

GALATIANS 6:1

The ability to restore another life is the revelation of His Truth living within us. It is the heart beat of all those who are coming to know and walk within the power and love of His Life. He is the restorer of my soul, and as He lives, so do all those who drink of the fountain of the living waters of His goodness and mercy. The measure of our walk and the validity of our following after Him is found in the sharing of His Life with others to restore, enable and exhort them to live Godly in Christ Jesus.

The Great Shepherd, who ever restores my life in Him, is to become in me a means of restoring others.

> "Christians are like the several flowers in a garden that have each of them the dew of heaven, which, being shaken with the wind, they let fall at each other's roots, whereby they are jointly nourished, and become nourishers of each other."
>
> JOHN BUNYAN

SELAH.

PSALM 23

Devotional Nine

THE PATHS OF RIGHTEOUSNESS

"He leads me in the paths of righteousness For His name's sake…"

PSALM 23:3

A path is not a destination. It is a way by which we travel to a specific destination. The **"paths of righteousness"** indicate a journey by which we travel to a desired end, a journey into Him who is Life. The concept of a journey, a life of growth and development, a goal that we are seeking to attain (Philippians 3:7–15), has been lost in the teaching of our day. Throughout the New Testament, we are exhorted to walk in righteousness, live in righteousness and **grow** in righteousness. Jesus tells us to "seek *first* the Kingdom of God and His righteousness". In other words, this should be the primary focus and desire of our hearts. We must see here that we are not just wandering in a religious wilderness filled with doctrines and concepts of

37

men in our search for righteousness. We are plainly told **He leads us** in the paths of this righteousness! To grow and live in the paths of righteousness is the result of following Him! It is a life of discovery, a life of His provisions, and a life filled with the wonder of Him who is The Life! Growth and development are the revelations of this Life. A life that is not growing and changing is a life that has become stagnant in its *heart*. It may breathe, may say all the right words, but in the very essence of its core it has "settled" in its quest for more of Him. This journey is one that causes us to become pilgrims concerning the things of this world. It causes us to ever be attentive to His voice and His direction. It is the governing principle by which we conduct ourselves in this world. It also causes us to be aware that we are a living part of all those who have gone before us; that in truth, we are the children of the promise, the true offspring of Abraham (Romans 9:8), who are looking and seeking for a City "whose builder and maker is GOD" (Hebrews 11:10).

> "These all died in faith, not having received the promises, but having seen them afar off were assured of them, **embraced them and confessed that they were strangers and pilgrims on the earth.** For those who say such things declare plainly that they seek a homeland"

HEBREWS 11:13 - 14

38

Reading the promises of God in the New Testament, we must realize there are tremendous promises yet unfulfilled. Such being the case, we are exhorted over and over to seek, pursue and "press toward the mark" for the attaining of these things. Should not that cry be found within our own hearts? The Way of God in Christ is a Way of life and wonder. It is a Way filled with change because it is a relationship with the infinite God of whom there is neither beginning nor ending. It is an eternal call, for no real and vital relationship ever ceases to grow and develop.

> "But the path of the just is as the shining light, that shineth MORE AND MORE unto the perfect day."

> PROVERBS 4:18

This path is filled with an ever growing light. This light beckons us on to greater things in Him and a desire to *participate* in the things He is doing. To touch the cry of His Heart for the life of another, to be co-laborers with Him in the development of life (His Life) in our brothers and sisters is a joy that is ours in Christ. How can we not "run with endurance" for the Joy of knowing and walking with Him? "For therein is the righteousness of God revealed from faith to faith" (ROMANS 1:16), describes a faith that is growing from one stage to another.

A people of the Way are ever on the move; they are

growing and they are discovering the bonds of relationship, the worth of knowing others who are also on this journey. The fruit of that fellowship is deep, powerful and filled with the pulsating life of the Son who is the author, sustainer and end of this journey!

> "The rung of a ladder was never meant to rest upon, but only to hold a man's foot long enough to enable him to put the other somewhat higher.

Thomas Henry Huxley (1825–1895)

SELAH.

PSALM 23

Devotional Ten

THE VALLEY OF THE SHADOW OF DEATH

"Yea, though I walk through the valley of the
shadow of death…"

PSALM 23:4

Throughout this Psalm we read of Him leading us to
places of quiet waters and green pastures and paths
of righteousness. Yet, in the midst of all this,
walking "through the valley of the shadow of
death…"! How can these things be? Is He not our
Shepherd? Is He not in charge and in control of all
the things going on around us? We are so struck
with the contrast and the suddenness of this verse
we rarely embrace its context within this Psalm. We
often hear it quoted because we see all around us
God's precious people walking in, enduring and
experiencing this valley that is to them the very
dark and real "shadow of death." How difficult it is
to relate this to the purposes of God, to relate this to
"Our Shepherd" in whom we are to place our

absolute trust. We question, we struggle and we wrestle with the "whys" and the "purposes" of such suffering, and often in these experiences, we know silence and a seeming sense of aloneness. It is here that we must draw upon His **character** and discover the "valley of the shadow of death" is really an extension of the "paths of righteousness," and He who loves us most is not deterred in His purpose to *make* us sons of God by causing us to walk in the same paths that His only begotten Son walked. He walked in them to "become" the Captain of our salvation (Hebrews 2:10); we walk in them to "attain" the reality of His life and salvation!

> "…that I may know Him and the power of His resurrection, and the fellowship of His sufferings, being conformed to His death, if, by any means, I may <u>attain</u> to the resurrection from the dead."

PHILIPPIANS 3:10

The "power of His resurrection" is the life that springs forth from identification with Him in His death. May God work in us the growing realization that the "valley of the shadow of death" is the doorway into the knowing of Him and the power of His resurrection! It is the means by which we experience the greatest depth of fellowship with and in Him! The life of the true Christian is one filled with contrast and contradiction; strength *out* of weakness, beauty *for* ashes, the oil of Joy *for* mourning, light shining *out* of darkness, victory *out* of seeming defeat, love *in* the midst of hatred, forgiveness *in* the face of atrocity and hate, and resurrection Life *out* of death! Who is sufficient for all these things? **Only JESUS, the risen Christ!** It is His Life in us that gives us hope for the dawn. It is His Life that is the resurrection Life, and as we walk in the "paths of righteousness," we are found walking in discovery that He is, in fact, "our hope of Glory."

The "valley of the shadow of death" is the way by which we come to know and trust in Him in all things. Such knowledge is not gained quickly; it is not learned by sermons and teachings; it can only be known by personal identification with Him who is "the Way, the Truth and the Life."

SELAH.

PSALM 23

Devotional Eleven

THE VALLEY OF THE SHADOW OF DEATH

"Yea, though I walk through the valley of the
shadow of death…"

PSALM 23:4

The Valley of the Shadow of Death is a place we
are to walk **through**. Valleys are places where our
vision is reduced, our world shrinks, we are
hemmed in by steep mountainsides and there is little
or no room for others. It is a place of walking
without being able to see, a place where the sun
rises late and sinks early, a place of darkness and
distress. It is here we also catch the fragrance of the
"Lily of the Valley," and though we cannot see
Him, there is a lingering sense that we are not far
from His care.

We all love the mountaintop experiences where our
vision expands and our faith soars as we see the

purposes of God in Christ. It is on the mountaintops that we see beyond where we now stand and the wind of His Spirit blows upon our face. The heart rises in eagerness to go from where we are to distant lands of promise, power and relationship. These are good moments and necessary ones as our Great Shepherd stirs our hearts to a greater longing for more of Him! It is these experiences that give us vision, but it is in the valleys that we **become** what we see from the heights. This journey of faith is one of becoming through identification with Him. Many love the teachings, the visionary aspects of the Christian landscape, but the Call Of God is one of picking up our cross and following Him! It is a life of discipline, a life of following the Lamb wherever He goes. It is not about us; it is about Him. It is the valley that separates the disciples from the adherents. It is the place of *becoming* where we learn in full measure that within ourselves dwells no good thing. In the learning of this, we begin to grasp the wonder and power of a love that surpasses understanding, a forgiveness that is unmerited, and a joy in God our Saviour.

It is in the Valleys that the metal is forged and faith becomes an unshakeable substance within the lives of those who would dare cross over. It is here the prisoner Joseph becomes "Zaphnath-Paaneah."

> "He sent a man before them, even Joseph, who was sold for a servant: Whose feet they hurt with fetters: he was laid in iron: Until the time that

46

his word came: the word of the
LORD tried him"

PSALM 105:18

Time is not sufficient to speak of the countless
others all over the world (even at this very moment)
who are enduring persecutions, trials, testings and
even death for His Name's sake. These valleys of
great sorrow and suffering, though grievous and
heartrending, are the means to new places of Life
within Him. It is the broken pitchers of Gideon's
army that revealed the inner light, causing the army
of Midian to flee and bringing great victory to the
people of God. **Those that are broken in the
hands of their God can never be broken by the
experiences of life**.

It is in the Valley of experience that the end of man
ushers in the strength and glory of God. It is here
we learn of a truth that His grace is sufficient!

The secret of the message of the valley is that we
walk through it. We do not succumb to it; we do not
spend our life sitting in it; we walk *through* it. We
keep moving, trusting, and walking until the Day
dawns and His Glory is seen!

Lord, we pray for the very substance of your faith to
empower, enlarge and encourage every one of your
people who at this moment are walking in the valley
of the shadow of death. We pray that the Glory of
who you are will be their Fortress, their Rock and

their High Tower in this time of need. May there be a new seeing of You, learning of You and worshiping of You that in the end of the journey may come forth the declaration of FAITH.

> "Great and marvelous are your works, Lord God Almighty! Just and true are Your ways, O King of the saints!"

REVELATION 15:2

SELAH.

PSALM 23

Devotional Twelve

FEAR

"I will fear no evil…"

PSALM 23:4

Fear is a common reality felt from the poorest of men to the richest. Fear, in itself, is not a sin. If fear were not a part of our everyday life, words such as courage, bravery, overcoming and fearless, among others, would have no value. It is what we **do** in the face of fear that determines whether a thing is commendable and worthy of honour or cowardly and worthy of shame. The Hebrew Word used here יָרֵא occurs hundreds of times in the Old Testament; here, as a verb, but also (though less often) as a noun and is used interchangeably to describe the Fear of the Lord or fear of a particular circumstance or situation. We read, throughout the Sacred Scriptures, of the Fear of the Lord being the principle part of Wisdom. We also read of those who, because of the fear of the Lord, obeyed Him, served Him and loved Him through the actions it produced in their lives.

In this Psalm, we read of an individual following and loving his/her Shepherd, and, in that following, find themselves walking through the valley of the Shadow of Death. It is in the midst of this experience we hear the declaration that they will not be deterred in following Him. The fear of this place of evil and darkness will not prevail or have any effect upon their decision to walk through this valley! These valleys are not crossed over because of the absence of fear; they are crossed over in spite of the fear! The love of God displaces the terror and the grip of fear, enabling us to pass over, to walk through, and to overcome the thing that would prevent us from obeying Him!

God's people should never feel ashamed when encountering fear; what matters is what we do in the face of it. Countless martyrs, throughout the ages, have faced the fear of torture, persecution and even death, yet they found the strength and the courage to be faithful to walk through the realities of these things. They are not moved by the fear because *He is with them..* There is a peace and a power that holds their souls in adversity, a presence that imparts Grace to stand, to walk and to hold the course in spite of all that rises up to meet them in the path of following Jesus.

> "…through whom also we have access **by faith** into this grace in

which we stand, and rejoice in hope of the glory of God. And not only that, but we also glory in tribulations, knowing that tribulation produces perseverance; and perseverance, character; and character, hope"

ROMANS 5:2-4

It is His Grace that enables us to stand, and this Grace is only accessed through the portal of Faith. Without faith, we have no access to this Grace. Grace not only to stand but to rejoice and glory in tribulation! Such things are too high for the ability of man within himself. These things are reserved for those who are growing in the seeking, pursuit and abiding in Him!

God has an answer to the fears that would cause us to falter in our way. His answer is Himself.

"I will fear no evil; For You are with me."

"Fear! His modus operandi is to manipulate you with the mysterious, to taunt you with the unknown. Fear of death, fear of failure, fear of God, fear of tomorrow—his arsenal is vast. His goal? To create cowardly, joyless souls. He doesn't want you to make the journey to the mountain. He figures if he can rattle you enough, you will take your eyes off the peaks and settle for a dull existence in the flatlands."

Max L. Lucado (1955–)

SELAH.

PSALM 23

Devotional Thirteen

HIS PRESENCE

"For Thou art with me"

PSALM 23:4

His Presence is the chief end and summation of all things. While some may seek recognition and the approval of men, a new generation is arising; one who will know the full purpose of God in Christ is to bring forth a people who live and walk in *His Presence.* The storm that is about to break upon our land in such fury and devastation will necessitate that deep place of abiding in Him. This is not a doctrinal statement; it must be the reality and truth of our everyday life. **He** is our Salvation, not a teaching or doctrine. To be a people of His Presence requires brokenness, humility and a heart that is compatible with His.

"…but to this man will I look, even
to him that is poor and of a contrite

spirit"

ISAIAH 66:2

If our inner life is right, there must always be a revelation of that in our daily life. What we are, we do. To be a people of His Presence, we must grow in truth inwardly and outwardly; the one must precede the other. Religion is only concerned with the outward; truth, to be truth, must become that in the secret places of our lives; "thou desirest truth **in** the inward parts" This is why righteousness is such a critical issue in this hour, as it can only be the offspring of a life that is growing in its submission to the leading and the purging of the Holy Spirit. Right thinking must produce right living.

> "LORD, who shall **abide** in thy tabernacle? who shall **dwell** in thy holy hill? He that walketh uprightly, and worketh righteousness, and speaketh the truth in his heart.He that backbiteth not with his tongue, nor doeth evil to his neighbour, nor taketh up a reproach against his neighbour. In whose eyes a vile person is contemned; but he honoureth them that fear the LORD. He that sweareth to his own hurt, and changeth not. He that putteth not out his money to usury, nor taketh reward against the innocent. He that **doeth** these things shall never be

moved."

PSALM 15:1–5

To Abide in Him is the longing of every true heart. This abiding in Him, growing in Him and living in Him requires a work of grace to bring forth the transformation necessary to live with Him in truth. How we need to grow in that sensitivity to the promptings and moving of His Spirit in our daily lives! Without obedience, this sensitivity can never be developed. May we become so His that we allow Him to interrupt our daily life to do His will, listen to His voice and be instructed in the way of His Life within us.

"Thou art with me" is more than a nice religious cliché; it must become the substance and the truth of who and what we are. To know of this Presence that enables us to walk through the valleys of difficulty, to become impervious to the fear of evil we must face, it is essential that we know He is with us! Our depth of abiding is revealed in the life that we live, how we treat others (especially those of the household of faith) and the thoughts and motivations of our hearts. It is a day to seek Him, a day to ask Him to search us and know us and to free us from the hidden things that offend in our lives.

"Blessed are the pure in heart for they **shall** see God"

"When we live in God's presence, when we are in the all for the All relationship, and surrender our own will and ways to God's will and ways, only then, no matter our physical and material circumstances, are we truly and fully alive. Only in God's presence are we able to enjoy the unique experience of holy freedom."

Brother Lawrence

"I will fear no evil for Thou art with me"

SELAH.

PSALM 23

Devotion Fourteen

THY ROD and THY STAFF

"Thy Rod and Thy staff they comfort me"

PSALM 23:4

The ministration of His Rod and His Staff are meant to have a profound effect upon our lives. We must realize *change* and *growth* are to be the normal Christian experience. The word in the Hebrew translated *"comfort"** here has a lot more to do with the ability ***"to be sorry, be moved to pity, have compassion"*** *(BDB Hebrew Definitions)* than with what our word comfort means in the English language.

This Hebrew Word is translated 104 times in the KJV; 67 times having to do with the various forms of the word comfort (comfort, comforteth, comforts, comforted….) and the majority of the remainder being translated in various forms of the word repent (repent, repenteth, repents, repenting…). Strong's concordance, when defining this word, says the following… *"A primitive root; properly to sigh, that is, breathe strongly; by implication to be sorry, that is, (in a favorable sense) to pity, console or (reflexively) rue."* The purpose of God working and transforming our lives is to **make us** men and women who reveal Him in truth and in character. The Rod and the Staff of the great Shepherd are to produce in us a condition of heart that reveals Him in the everyday outflow of our lives. Without **becoming,** our lives will always be an act of trying to "appear" righteous; a labour of great and continual effort to show a semblance of righteousness rather than simply being the real thing.

The Rod and Staff are the tools of the One loving Shepherd. They are both manifestations of the same Heart and, in fact, the Rod is also the Staff. It is how it is used that determines its expression. The same gracious God who administers correction is the same one who heals, restores and leads us to "green pastures," "quiet waters" and in the "paths of righteousness."

All of God's dealings with us are to one end: to make us expressions of His Glory by what we are. It is in becoming His righteousness that we can, in fact, do righteousness. Therefore, we do not faint in His dealings with us for that is the only means by which we may grow.

Those who see the purposes of God in the daily grind of life are able to find the grace to submit themselves under the "mighty hand of God" and thereby profit in wisdom, understanding, and the character development necessary in this journey.

The true purpose of teaching is to produce right thinking, and right thinking must bring forth right living. The scriptures declare that we are to be "transformed **by** the renewing of our **minds**". Unless the ministry of truth is producing change within the people of God it is a vain thing. Faith comes by hearing, and by faith alone will this life of *becoming* be possible. The Rod and the Staff are the instruments of the Great Shepherd to work in us the discipline and the guidance necessary for us to grow in Him.

Hebrews says, "For whom the Lord loveth he chasteneth, and scourgeth every son whom he receiveth. If ye endure chastening, God dealeth with you as with sons; for what son is he whom the father chasteneth not?" There is great comfort in knowing there is One who watches over us to ever bring correction and guidance into our lives. The fruit of such knowledge is confidence and peace.

> "In the destiny of every moral being, there is an object more worthy of God than happiness. It is character. And the grand aim of man's creation is the development of a grand character, and grand character is, by its very nature, the product of probationary **discipline**."

Austin Phelps

* Note: "**H5162.** נָחַם *nāḥam:* A verb meaning to be sorry, to pity, to comfort, to avenge. The verb often means to be sorry or to regret: the Lord was sorry that He had made people (Gen. 6:6); He led Israel in a direction to avoid war when they left Egypt, lest they became so sorry and grieved that they would turn back (Ex. 13:17). The Lord had compassion on His people (i.e., He became sorry for them because of the oppression their enemies placed on them [Judg. 2:18]). While the Lord could be grieved, He did not grieve or become sorry so that He changed His mind as a human does (1 Sam. 15:29). The word also means to comfort or console oneself. Isaac was comforted after Sarah, his mother, died (Gen. 24:67)"

THE COMPLETE WORD STUDY DICTIONARY: OLD TESTAMENT Warren Baker, D.R.E. Eugene Carpenter, Ph.D.

SELAH.

PSALM 23

Devotional Fifteen

THE NECESSITY OF HIS ROD

"Thy Rod…comforts* me"

PSALM 23:4

Freedom, Peace and Confidence are not possible without authenticity. Authenticity is the result of truth. Truth, by its very nature, must reveal and make manifest that which is false and superficial. Men may have knowledge and information concerning God without ever touching the *Truth* of God, for it is this that reveals all untruths. A person can have great understanding of the scriptures and yet be totally blind to the true condition of his or her heart. This is deception of the highest order. It is called "religion" and never are we more susceptible to deception than within the realms of "religious truth." Instead of the scriptures penetrating our hearts with the Holy gaze of His Presence, we use them to "support" our own agendas, weaknesses and carnality. We use them as a cloak to hide ourselves from the very truth that was meant to deliver us. It is only when we are honest in heart that the Word of God uncovers and frees us from all that would hinder us in our growth and desire to see Him. Purity of heart is the pre-requisite of seeing Him!

> "For the word of God *is* living and powerful, and sharper than any two-edged sword, piercing even to the division of soul and spirit, and of joints and marrow, and is a discerner of the thoughts and intents of the heart."

HEBREWS 4:12

Authenticity (true being) is not the result of a man being true to himself but rather the fruit of a life that, by God's Grace, has become **true in God**. It is in the seeing of Him that I know myself (see Isaiah 6, Revelation 1:12–17 and many others). He is the Truth, and it is in the seeing of Him alone that we are changed from the corrupted Adam into His likeness!

> "But we all, with unveiled face, beholding as in a mirror the glory of the Lord, are being transformed into the same image from glory to glory, just as by the Spirit of the Lord."

II CORINTHIANS 3:18

The ability to understand and see truth is an issue of the heart, not of the intellect. Therefore, not only are we unable to see truth by our own efforts, we, by nature, hate truth because truth is that which exposes the "untrueness" of all that we are (see John 16:18). When Jesus said, "I AM The Way, The Truth...," He revolutionized the definition of truth. The religious Pharisees considered truth in terms of having knowledge of the scriptures; because of that they could not see Him, who is the truth, standing before them. Of them, Jesus said:

> "You search the Scriptures, for in them you think you have eternal life; and these are they which testify of Me."

> JOHN 5:39

My knowing of HIM (who is Truth) is directly related to the degree I truly know and see myself in the light of Him.

> "...but then shall I know even as also I am known."

> I CORINTHIANS 13:12

It is because of these things that the Rod of our Great Shepherd is so important in the development of our life with Him. There are times when I have missed God. I have misinterpreted His will and purpose for me, and it was His mercy that prevented me from walking in the error of my own wrongness.

David declares, in Psalm 119, *"Before I was afflicted I went astray: but now have I kept thy word,"* and again, *"It is good for me that I have been afflicted; that I might learn thy statutes,"* and yet again, *"I know, O LORD, that thy judgments are right, and that thou in faithfulness hast afflicted me"*! Our God is Faithful, Merciful and True, and how vital it is that we acknowledge our need for His correction, rebuke, reproof and discipline in our lives. For all His dealings with us are to the end that, **"we may be partakers of His Holiness!"**

Men who are only interested in being right will never be able to receive correction or instruction. In reality they do not have a Love for Truth. In fact, (as of old) they have a desire for knowledge and understanding that can be used to support their agendas and their way of living. Clearly have the scriptures declared there are people who are *"Ever learning, and never able to come to the knowledge of the truth."*

It is in our journey into the discovery of Him that we learn, in truth, who we really are. This is a journey filled with much correction and discipline, but it is as we receive these expressions of His love that we are made soft and pliable in His hands. It is here we grow in mercy and brokenness before Him and tremble at His word. These are the fruits produced by His Rod in our lives and the essential quality of heart that is greatly desired by our Heavenly Father!

"...but to this man will I look, even to him that is poor and of a contrite spirit, and trembleth at my word."

ISAIAH 66:2

"When a man's heart is right with God, the mysterious utterances of the Bible are spirit and life to him. Spiritual truth is discernible only to a pure heart, not to a keen intellect. It is not a question of profundity of intellect, but of purity of heart."

Oswald Chambers

* See PSALM 23, Devotional Twelve for the definition of the Hebrew word used here.

SELAH.

PSALM 23

Devotional Sixteen

CORRECTION AND GROWTH

"Thy Rod...comforts* me"

PSALM 23:4

Without correction and accountability, personal growth and fruitfulness become stagnated and stunted. Men who refuse correction cease to grow and cease to live. Jesus said "every *branch* that bears fruit He prunes, that it may bear more fruit." This truth is aptly revealed in the world around us. Everything concerning life needs to be channeled in order to have direction and purpose. A river without banks is a flood; electricity without a path and a purpose we call "static"; and a believer in God who has no personal vision or "mark" (Philippians 3:14) is one who will be without discipline or purpose. A good landscaper prunes his garden that it may grow and become all he has purposed and envisioned it to be when he planted it. Jesus said His father was the Vinedresser, and they that are of this Vine (Jesus) are to bear fruit that the Father may be glorified.

Therefore, Fruit is anything that pleases and glorifies the Father.

It is in us *receiving* of His correction that we grow in fruitfulness and the inherent ability to bring forth expressions of the Son to glorify the Father. Let us hear the admonition from God's Word; "My son, do not despise the chastening of the Lord, Nor detest His correction; For whom the Lord loves He corrects, Just as a father the son *in whom* he delights." (Proverbs 3:11–12) The proof of God's Love and His ongoing investment into our lives is revealed in His Rod. We read In the Old and New Testaments of the evident Hand of God actively expressing His Love and correction in the lives of people; some were *exercised* by it and others refused it with eternal consequences. Men who refuse correction choose a life that eventually comes to ruin. God's Word has summed up this truth in one powerful verse:

> "He who keeps instruction (Hebrew: correction) is in the way of life, But he who refuses correction goes astray."

PROVERBS 10:17

Does this not explain the apostasy in our land today? Is there not a reason that the love of many have grown cold and indifferent? People are content to go through the motions of religion while failing to realize that we are here to **bear fruit** unto Him who has called us out of darkness into His Light.

God's Word to His people today is one of grave importance; one that reveals and lays bare the reason we are in such disarray, impotence and apathy:

> "I have even sent to you all My servants the prophets, daily rising up early and sending *them.* Yet they did not obey Me or incline their ear, but stiffened their neck. This *is* a nation that does not obey the voice of the Lord their God nor receive correction. Truth has perished and has been cut off from their mouth."

JEREMIAH 7:25-28

It is a Day for us to turn, to receive correction and to be *exercised* in it that we may come forth as Gold tried in the Fire; purified and freed from our own agendas to do His will that there may be Glory and Honour in His House.

King David knew well the power of change and repentance found in the ministration of truth from others in His day and the fruit that comes from the receiving of it.

"Let the righteous strike me; It shall be a kindness. And let him rebuke me: It shall be as excellent oil; Let my head not refuse it."

PSALM 141:5

"Cheap grace is the preaching of forgiveness without requiring repentance, baptism without church discipline, Communion without confession, absolution without personal confession. Cheap grace is grace without discipleship, grace without the cross, grace without Jesus Christ."

Dietrich Bonhoeffer

* See PSALM 23, Devotional Twelve for the definition of the Hebrew word used here.

SELAH.

PSALM 23

Devotional Seventeen

THY STAFF

"Thy STAFF…comforts* me"

PSALM 23:4

The Hebrew Word translated here as staff has two meanings. The first is translated generally as anything that supports and stabilizes *(A feminine noun indicating a support, a supply. It is used for what firms up, keeps stable, furnishes needed supplies {TCWS of the Old Testament})*. It is this aspect that causes us to trust in Him, lean upon Him and draw from Him strength for all our daily needs. On our journey of Life we discover the truth of all He is to us. Through this unseen support and ministration, we began to see He is not only our Saviour but indeed He is our salvation on a daily basis. It is in the present truth of His life that we find ourselves in full agreement with Psalm 46:1: He is our **present help** in trouble. He is not a God that is far off, but a God who is present and real. It is this present help that comforts us, humbles us and causes us to exclaim with the writer of the Book of Hebrews, "what is man that thou art mindful of him or the son of man that thou shouldst visit him". These are the moments when His unmerited goodness causes us to be humbled and broken, His goodness expressed in the face of our stubbornness and pride.

His staff supports, leads and guides, gently nudging us into the path that He has chosen. It is His staff that leads us to green pastures, quiet waters and causes us to know He is ever watching over the lives of His own. How good and faithful is our Shepherd. How merciful and gracious are His ways with us. Left to ourselves, we are all like sheep that "have wandered astray." We have sought out our own ways, our own pastures, and without Him, we would ever be lost in the wilderness of our own wisdom with our own miserable resources. The Lord is our Shepherd and in the ministration of His staff we are comforted and made right. It gives us hope and comfort when we feel the sting of His correction, for it is in learning of Him that we grow in the wisdom and love of our shepherd. It is in learning of Him that we can be more effective in our ministration of that life to one another. For the Body of Christ to become One in heart, faith and reality, there must be a corporate expression of His heart to one another. It is in learning of Him that we are no longer able to segregate ourselves from each other. For to have the Love of God beating in our hearts, we must come to the place of loving what He loves and hating what He hates. We can no longer pick and choose who may be our brother or sister. We can no longer elevate one ministry over and above another, for we have seen that each ministration of His life is necessary to reveal His fullness.

It is in being humbled by His goodness we become expressions of that goodness to one another. It is in the appreciation of His unmerited grace we become expressions of that grace to those around us. The truth of the staff enables us to no longer walk in the poverty of our own resources. Rather, it brings us to the recognition of a supply of strength that is beyond ourselves, a strength to stand when we have no strength, a hope in His supply that will not allow us to succumb to the testings we must endure. His staff becomes a point of strength where we can declare the "The Lord is my Shepherd, I shall not lack…" He is come to be to us all that our present circumstances require. We are not to feel as chaff driven by the wind; we are not to feel as sheep having no shepherd; and we are not to be as orphans without hope in this world. He has come to strengthen us in Him, to bring us to a place of trust in the God of our provision. He has come to make us partakers of the riches of His Father's house!

His staff comforts us, enables us and causes us to become rich in the provisions of our God.

"The LORD God is my strength, and he will make my feet like hinds' feet, and he will make me to walk upon mine high places."

HABBAKUK 3:19

* See PSALM 23, Devotional Twelve for the definition of the Hebrew Word used here.

SELAH.

PSALM 23

Devotional Eighteen

THE KING'S TABLE

"Thou preparest a table before me... "

PSALM 23:5

The table spoken of here is no ordinary table; it is the King's Table. It is the Table of Royalty designated for Kings, yet we find it set for those who follow the Shepherd! The Hebrew Word translated "table" * here is properly defined as *"a king's table, (for) private use, sacred uses"* (BDB Hebrew Definitions). It is the Hebrew Word used for the "Table of Show Bread"; the Hebrew word used when the Queen of Sheba visited Solomon's "Table" and was astonished at the glory found there. It is used when God was angry at Israel for how they treated His Table in their day of apostasy and neglect (see Malachi 1:7, 12). This is the Table that is provided to all who would follow their Shepherd and their King! It is a table of provision, a table of intimate and private concourse with the King of Kings. It is here we eat of the Hidden

Manna. It is here that He comes and draws us aside to break the bread of fellowship and understanding that we may grow in strength and in our relationship with Him. This is a *private* table reserved for those who follow Him in Spirit and Truth, not with lip service but with all the passion of a heart that knows nothing but Jesus can satisfy the longing within.

This is a prepared table. It is not one that is hastily set. The Hebrew word used here for "prepared" is translated most often in the Old Testament speaking of the armies of Israel being "arrayed" for battle. It is a prepared table for a prepared people. It is ordered and set with the utmost of care and attention to detail. God is never in a hurry. He is always the One in control, and His Table is prepared from eternity for our strengthening and preparation. While men would panic in the Day of Battle, our God is calm and purposed. We see Jesus at the last supper with His disciples, knowing full well the drama that was about to unfold, filled with peace and enjoying intimate fellowship with His disciples! There was no panic, for He was and is the reigning One! Let us draw near to this table and eat of Him, with Him and by Him that we may nourished and ready to meet the enemy of our day.

This private table is seen throughout the Gospels as Jesus spoke in parables to the crowds and the religious leaders. Later, He would take His Disciples aside to make sure they knew and understood the truths of what He had spoken. It is in these private moments that the "bread of Life" becomes alive to our hearts and we see and hear things in a new way! The reason men do not feel the power of His Life pulsating in the Word of God is that they have not discovered this table. This table will only be found by those "who follow the Lamb" wherever He goes. This is a table of relationship prepared for those who would eat of its rich provisions and walk in the strength of it. It is not a Table filled with sweet things only, but also with meat, seasoned with bitter herbs, and bread to make men strong (EXODUS 12:8). It is, after all, the "Table of the Lord," and those who would minister Him must eat **all** that is set before them; it is in the eating of Him that He becomes a part of us!

> "Verily, verily, I say unto you, Except ye eat the flesh of the Son of man, and drink his blood, ye have no life in you. Whoso eateth my flesh, and drinketh my blood, hath eternal life; and I will raise him up at the last day. For my flesh is meat indeed, and my blood is drink indeed. He that eateth my flesh, and drinketh my blood, dwelleth in me, and I in him. As the living Father hath sent me, and I live by the Father: so he that eateth me, even he shall live by me."

JOHN 6:52 - 57

This is not a table for the curious, for those who like to hear the latest teaching or those who run after signs and wonders. Rather, it is a table set aside for those who will eat of Him through the medium of *obedience*! Martyrs and Saints of all generations have eaten of this table and found Faith and Grace to overcome. May we follow the Lamb, in our day, to share at His table the prepared provision for the day that is upon us.

> "...To him that overcometh will I give to eat of the hidden manna."

> REVELATION 2:17

> "God walks with the humble; He reveals himself to the lowly; He gives understanding to the little ones; He discloses his meaning to pure minds, but hides His grace from the curious and the proud."

> THOMAS A KEMPIS

* **Note,** the instances where this word is used, consistently refer to a table of royalty (good and bad), prophets and a table of showbread in the Tabernacle and Temples.

table, 56 Ex 25:23, Ex 25:27-28 (2), Ex 25:30, Ex 26:35 (3), Ex 30:27, Ex 31:8, Ex 35:13, Ex 37:10, Ex 37:14-16 (3), Ex 39:36, Ex 40:4, Ex 40:22, Ex 40:24, Lev 24:6, Num 3:31, Judg 1:7 (2), 1 Sam 20:29, 1 Sam 20:34, 2 Sam 9:7, 2 Sam 9:10-11 (2), 2 Sam 9:13, 2 Sam 19:28, 1 Kin 2:7, 1 Kin 4:27, 1

Kin 7:48, 1 Kin 10:5, 1 Kin 13:20, 1 Kin 18:19, 2 Kin 4:10, 1 Chr 28:16, 2 Chr 9:4, 2 Chr 13:11, 2 Chr 29:18, Neh 5:17, Ps 23:5, Ps 69:22, Ps 78:19, Ps 128:3, Prov 9:2, Isa 21:5, Isa 65:11, Ezek 23:41, Ezek 39:20, Ezek 41:22, Ezek 44:16, Dan 11:27, Mal 1:7, Mal 1:12

tables, 14 1 Chr 28:16 (2), 2 Chr 4:8, 2 Chr 4:19, Isa 28:8, Ezek 40:39-43 (9)

The Book of Hebrews declares, "We have an altar from which those who serve the tabernacle have no right to eat..." (Hebrews 13:10) The only way to eat of this table is to Serve and Follow the Lamb of God!

SELAH.

PSALM 23

Devotional Nineteen

THE PLACE OF FEASTING

"Thou preparest a table before me in the presence of mine enemies"

PSALM 23:5

This table has been set with rich provisions and is there for us to eat and drink and become strong thereby. It is not a table for mere talking and listening, but it is the table of the Bread of His Life which must be consumed in order that it becomes a reality in our lives. We have had much in terms of teaching; in fact, much of our Christian experience in this land is really one of *listening* to didactical teaching and the dissemination of information. It becomes an intellectual exercise and much of it remains purely theoretical in its actual application. We have become good at hearing, debating, and discussing the doctrines and concepts of men without the substance of *living* the reality of the Life of Christ. The outward form of teaching is necessary for a season but, somewhere, it must give way to the experience and walk in every true disciple. Notice, this Table of Provision is not set in a nice and comfortable Christian setting but in the presence of our enemies! The provision comes as we overcome our enemies.

In the conflicts of life, we discover His strength. Here, as the Word of God is eaten and made real, we no longer live in ethereal teachings, concepts and good sounding religious ideas. Instead, His Life is discovered *within* the conflicts of our daily lives! We discover the wonder of a living Faith that must bring what we have heard into our walk! This is where Christ becomes the experience of the individual believer. By its very nature, the life of overcoming can only be appropriated on an individual basis. The corporate expression is only as valid as the authenticity of the individual. Just because I *listen* to good teaching does not mean my Christian experience is valid. The validity of my Life in Christ can only be known by the expression of His Life in me. For that to be the truth of my life requires not only a hearing of His Word but it must give way to a doing of that Word. Obedience is the way to the life of overcoming. If there is no obedience, there can be no overcoming!

In the Gospels, we see and hear Jesus teaching the Word concerning the Kingdom of God, and we are struck with the wonder and the wisdom found in the beauty of His words. However, He does not allow the disciples to linger in the hearing only. Because He is not just a teacher, (but has come to fulfill His

Father's will) He instructs the disciples to live and walk out that which He has spoken. He sends them out to heal the sick, cast out demons and to declare the Word of the Kingdom! Likewise, the Word must become flesh in our own experience. We must eat of the provisions of this table in the presence of our enemies; not only the obvious, external ones, but more importantly, the enemies of our heart, the weaknesses of our flesh and the "I" that is always clamoring for pre-eminence, comfort and its own way. We must find Him as our victory here, or it will matter very little what we know. Judas heard and saw the Glory of Christ, yet in the end, he betrayed Him. It is not enough to know and have an association with Jesus; we must *eat of Him* at this table prepared for us in the "presence of our enemies"!

Men love knowledge and understanding. We love to discuss things, debate things and share things, but Jesus came that men may have "Life and Life abundantly". He did not come to bring a new teaching or to tickle men's ears with revelatory speech. He came to be the very image of all that God is, not an image only but the *means* by which the fallen race of man could become the **Body of Christ** in the earth. For this reason, He sets this table of provision that we may become bone of His bone and flesh of His flesh in demonstration in our daily life. It is crucial we see that the conflicts and tribulations of this life are given to us to make us become strong. May God save us from teachings that leave us impoverished, impotent and unable to walk, and may we find His table prepared for us in the presence of our enemies.

> Obstacles in the pathway of the weak become stepping-stones in the pathway of the strong.

Thomas Carlyle (1795–1881)

SELAH.

PSALM 23

Devotional Twenty

BREAD FOR US

"Thou preparest a table before me in the presence of mine enemies"

PSALM 23:5

"They are bread for us". This was the declaration of Faith that characterized the lives of Joshua and Caleb in the face of Israel's unbelief as they realized the number and the size of the enemies that inhabited the Land of Promise. Their strength was not in themselves. Their confidence was grounded in the unshakable trust that God was with them and therefore the size and scope of their enemies was irrelevant. This is the crucial element to a faithful and consistent walk in God. The key phrase to this declaration is found in the verse preceding, **"If the Lord delight in us."** True vision always lifts our eyes from ourselves and causes us to focus on the things that please Him. The life of the Son was

always centered upon the one and great eternal desire to please the Father. He was fixed upon this one thing and as a result His life was governed by that *One Great Will.* The ability to see our enemies as bread for us is in direct correlation to our submission to His purposes. We are here to **do** His will and to **walk** in His ways regardless of the cost.

> "The secret of the LORD is with them that fear him; and he will show them his covenant."

PSALM 25:14

The life of feasting at this table must always be preceded by the Altar; *the Altar of Burnt Offering precedes the Table of Showbread.* Vision is the result of a man's walk. Our ability to see and understand the purposes of God is directly related to our heart's condition, not our intellect. Spiritual ignorance is the fruit of disobedience. It was in the obedience of Abraham to take his only son Isaac and offer him unto the Lord (as per the Word of the Lord) that Abraham saw the revelation of "Jehovah Jireh" (Genesis 22:13). It was *when* the feet of the Priests carrying the Ark stepped into the flooding river Jordan that it parted, allowing them to enter the Promised Land. It was *when* Judah offered himself in the stead of Benjamin that Joseph could no longer restrain himself from revealing who he was in their midst. Joseph was there the whole time, yet they could not see him until there was a change of heart. So too, this table is set before us with the bountiful provisions of our God to nourish and supply us with all that we need to finish this race "that is set before us" (HEBREWS 12:1).

"Thou hast enlarged me when I was in distress"

PSALM 4:1

"It is only by obedience that we understand the teaching of God."

Oswald Chambers (1874–1917)

"Every man must tread the Word for himself. One may read it in one shape, another in another: all will be right if it be indeed the Word they read, and they read it by the lamp of obedience. He who is willing to do the will of the Father shall know the truth...the Spirit is "given to them that obey him."

GEORGE MACDONALD

SELAH.

PSALM 23

Devotional Twenty-One

HIS ANOINTING

"Thou anointest my head with oil"

PSALM 23:5

In the Old Testament, three expressions were anointed in God's people: Priests, Kings and Prophets. These were to be holy expressions necessary for the ministration of God's Laws, His Mercy and His Council. This anointing was to sanctify, empower and to declare the calling of God upon a man for God's specific purposes.

> "...thou shalt anoint unto Me him whom I name unto thee."

1 SAMUEL 16:3

The anointing is to bring forth a life that is lived **unto** Him. It is to work in and saturate a man's life until his whole being is lived **unto** the Lord. It is a most significant sign of a life that has been chosen by God to be lived **unto** God for His own end. We read of this same thing in the New Testament.

> "But ye shall receive power, after that the Holy Ghost is come upon you: and ye shall be witnesses **unto Me** both in Jerusalem, and in all Judaea, and in Samaria, and unto the uttermost part of the earth."

ACTS 1:8

This anointing has come to all those who have been washed in the precious blood of the Lamb, all who have sought for and desired a Life of separation by seeking and desiring the Baptism of the Holy Spirit. This is not to live a life unto ourselves or to seek to build up a church or ministry but to be witnesses **unto Him**! It is to live our daily lives with a cry within our hearts for Him to "work in us to will and to **do** of His good pleasure," that we might truly know of the Joy of the Lord (His Joy) welling up in our lives.

"Thou anointest my head with oil" is more than just a poetic phrase. It is a substantial reality necessary for any life to live and be equipped to walk in the Way of the Son. This anointing is an essential step in the journey of a life that no longer desires anything but Him and no longer finds satisfaction in anything else. This anointing brings a realization that in every place and in every moment, He is watching us and knows our thought life; our motivations and our actions are weighed in the balances of His righteousness. There is a sobering awareness that we are in truth "witnesses unto Him"!

This anointing welcomes the search light of truth to every corner of our own hearts. It matters very little what men think or say, for we have discovered the reason for living is to please and glorify Him; to know Him more and more in this brief journey of life.

This anointing also causes us to speak truth and to become more true ourselves. It is because of this anointing men can be empowered to become Priests, Kings and Prophets unto God. It is because of His call, His Power and His Mercy that ordinary men and women become authentic expressions of the Most High God!

We need look no further than the young child David to see the effect of this anointing as he grew into the call and purposes of God as a King, a Priest and a Prophet. Can we not expect greater things from a New Covenant that has made provision for our sin by the precious blood of the spotless Lamb?

> "For the law made nothing perfect, but the bringing in of a better hope did; by the which we draw nigh unto God."

HEBREWS 7:19

He has brought forth a New and Living ministration

91

of the Life of the Son that we might live in the glorious provision of His anointing! He **is** come, and the scriptures testify we **have** received of this anointing that we might be taught of Him and empowered of Him to become witnesses of His Life in this world.

> "But the anointing which ye have received of him abideth in you. The Holy Spirit is the gift of the Risen Christ. His anointing filling, empowering work is a baptism of love that gives power to make Jesus real to you and known to others."

Winkie Prateny

SELAH.

PSALM 23

Devotional Twenty-Two

HIS ANOINTING OIL

"Thou anointest my head with oil"

PSALM 23:5

The anointing brings sanctification, power and ability. It takes ordinary people and empowers them to be expressions of Glory and manifests the gifts and the calling of a merciful and Most High God. There is, however, more to this anointing than power and divine enablement; empowered vessels can still be selfish and wounded. They can be carnal, absorbed with self, deceived and fragile. It is necessary for us to know and understand the full work of God is to *make* us, in thought, word and deed, a people who *are* like Him!

> "And hath **made** us kings and priests unto God…."

REVELATION 1:6

The Hebrew Word,* translated "oil" in this verse, denotes fatness, richness, with clear references to cleansing and healing. In order for us to be made rich and fat in the blessings of our God, we must become whole within the very heart of our being. Without the healing and cleansing aspect of the work of the Holy Spirit, we would be blemishes to all that God has purposed man should be. The scriptures are full of examples of men and women who have power without character and the resulting horror of such things. **Power without character is the great evil in the world today, whether it be political, financial, judicial, or, above all, religious.**

It is interesting to see that the express meaning of the word used in the Hebrew for oil conveys the essential purpose of God in His plan of redemption and salvation. It is to be unto us the power of God working to bring forth of His richness, His abundance and His enablement to shine forth the character, the person and the heart of the amointed One, Christ Jesus our Lord! Within the flow of the Life of the Son in us, that power (**dunamis** Greek) is active and alive to transform the fallen sons of Adam into the Children of God!

Let us not become discouraged in His dealings with us. Let us realize that while much of the "Christian" world may seek power, signs and wonders, there is a quiet and determined work of the Holy Spirit to bring us to the place of being vessels fit and prepared for the Master's use; vessels that know the deep cost of walking in forgiveness, knowing how to extend mercy to others, having peace in the midst of conflict, showing grace for others, and clinging to truth regardless of the consequences! These vessels are shaped by a true knowing of themselves and their struggles, and because of that knowledge they see and understand others more clearly. They have been freed from the bitterness and strife within their own hearts that the sweetness of His healing waters may flow. In all of these things, we *become* approved unto our God. It is as the anointing oil has its way within the very recesses of our hearts that we know of His Joy and approval in our lives.

II Timothy says,

> "But in a great house there are not only vessels of gold and of silver, but also of wood and of earth; and some to honour, and some to dishonour. If a man therefore purge himself from these, he shall be a vessel unto honour, sanctified, and meet for the master's use, and prepared unto every good work."

II TIMOTHY 2:20-21

To that end, let us run the race that is set before us that we might be vessels of honour, sanctified and ready for the Master's use.

> "The baptism of the Holy Ghost makes us witnesses to Jesus, not

wonder-workers. The witness is not
to what Jesus does, but to what He
is."

Oswald Chambers (1874–1917)

* *"שֶׁמֶן A masculine noun meaning fat, oil. This
word has a wide range of figurative meanings
relating to richness and plenty. Most simply, it is
used of food, relating to feasts of good, rich food
(Isa. 25:6). It is also used frequently of oil. This can
be oil used for food and cooking (Deut. 8:8; 32:13);
for oil which was used to anoint holy objects or
kings (Ex. 30:25; 1 Sam. 10:1); or for oil used as an
ointment to soothe and cleanse, leading to healing
(Ps. 133:2; Isa. 1:6). The figurative meanings are
also important. This word can be used to signify
strength, such as in Isaiah 10:27 where growing fat
meant growing strong. It also frequently relates to
fruitfulness and fertile places where good things
grew (Isa. 5:1; 28:1). The overall picture one gets
from this word is that of richness, strength, and
fertility."*

THE COMPLETE WORD STUDY DICTIONARY:
OLD TESTAMENT; Warren Baker, D.R.E. Eugene
Carpenter, Ph.D.

SELAH.

PSALM 23

Devotional Twenty-Three

HIS ABUNDANCE

"my cup runneth over"

PSALM 23:5

The overflowing cup is a result of the Anointing. This life of abundance and flow is the result of His Life and His influence in our lives. Man, left to himself, is a desert, an unruly patch of weeds, thorns and thistles. The only hope of Glory for any man is "Christ **in** us". This abundant flow of the grace of God is known, along with the keen recognition, that within ourselves we are barren and impoverished. Only He has the ability to make the desert bloom, the barren land a fruitful field and the fountains of living water flow without measure. Many of God's people spend so much time focusing on their lack and their own condition that they remove themselves from the fountain of His abundance. We need to take note of the Word of God in this regard.

"He that believeth on me, as the scripture hath said, out of his belly shall flow rivers of living water. But this spake he of the Spirit, <u>which they that believe on him should receive</u>: for the Holy Ghost was not yet given...."

JOHN 7:38 - 39

The flow of this river, out of the lives of His people, is based not only on the Holy Spirit being given but also being received! There is much emphasis on sending men and women to Bible schools, conferences and seminars when the real need is to see them filled and empowered to live in the vitality of the Holy Spirit! Teaching will not empower a man (as good and as necessary as it is). True teaching must bring the people of God into the place of receiving the reality of His Spirit to live this abundant life.

Christians are not to be impoverished, selfish, carnal and wounded people. They are to be living epistles of the living God. It is as the world reads these "living epistles" that they will know and glorify our Father Who is in heaven.

> "Let your light so shine before men,
> that they may see your good works,
> and glorify your Father which is in
> heaven."

MATTHEW 5:16

True light produces True Works! The pouring out of the Holy Spirit is to produce something far higher, far deeper and far more comprehensive than merely speaking in tongues. It is to produce a life teeming with the grace and glory of God, a life that bears fruit in every circumstance, a life that can identify with the pain and suffering of others, a life of abundance that flows out to others with the faith and mercy of our great God. It is to be a life that stands for truth and God's way, in a day of growing darkness and apostasy, with a boldness to declare the purposes of God regardless of the consequences. Such things are only ours through a life that has received, and continues to receive, the pouring forth of this unmerited gift of the Holy Spirit.

Let us never stop growing and living and seeking and desiring more of all He desires to give, for we are reminded that the Spirit of God is poured out without measure! It is we who determine the depth of its influence and Lordship in our lives; it is we who must ask, must knock, must seek this anointing that is now ours because Jesus has been Glorified! (John 7:39)

This Gift is given not on the basis of our own merit,

but *because Jesus has been glorified*! The abundance, the life of overflowing is ours because of His merit and His Ascension.

> "Wherefore he saith, When he ascended up on high, he led captivity captive, and gave gifts unto men."

EPHESIANS 4:8

Let us re-evaluate the measure of the life we live today as compared to the purpose God has for us in Christ Jesus our Lord.

> "Amplius" means broader, fuller, wider. That is God's perpetual word to us in relation to filling of the Holy Spirit. We can never have enough to satisfy His yearning desire. When we have apprehended most, there are always unexpected supplies in store ready to be drawn upon."

FB Meyer

SELAH.

PSALM 23

Devotional Twenty-Four

SURELY

"Surely goodness and mercy shall follow me all the days of my life"

PSALM 23:6

Surely! The word used for "surely" is a particle of affirmation in the Hebrew language; it indicates a certainty! It is the declaration of Faith arising from a heart that is following after the Great Shepherd! It is a declaration from a life that knows there will be "valleys of shadows" and separation, of difficulties that seem insurmountable and too deep to cross in our own strength. It is the assurance felt within the heart of one who knows the character and the grace of our God. It is the very thing that carries us through the great trials and troubles we encounter in this life. This confidence is not borne of a confidence in ourselves but is founded upon His **Goodness** and **Mercy** that is ours as we pursue and follow after Him! We see this same declaration echoed in the life of Paul and others in the New

Testament.

> "Yet in all these things we are more than conquerors through Him who loved us. For I am <u>persuaded</u> that neither death nor life, Nor angels nor principalities nor powers, Nor things present nor things to come, Nor height nor depth, nor any other created thing shall be able to separate us From the love of God which is in Christ Jesus our Lord."

ROMANS 8:37-39

This surety must come from a life of knowing and doing. True confidence is the fruit of doing. While men may say and declare great things, it is through those who do His Will that the quiet fruit of confidence and stability is revealed.

> "And wisdom and knowledge shall be the stability of thy times, *and* strength of salvation: the fear of the LORD *is* his treasure."

ISAIAH 33:6

"Surely" is the positive declaration of those who have followed their Shepherd throughout the journey of life. For in the following of Him we can be assured that His Goodness and Mercy *will* follow us; like a boat crossing a lake it leaves a wake that goes out to distant shores. The Psalmist here declares that the wake of God's Goodness and Mercy will "surely" touch others, bless others and make known to others the Goodness of our God. We are not here to become obsessed with watching our wake! In so doing we take our eyes off Him and quickly become lost in the wilderness of self. It is in keeping our eyes upon Him and following Him that we can be confident of this very thing: His Goodness and Mercy will follow us.

"SURELY goodness and mercy shall follow me all the days of my life"

SELAH.

PSALM 23

Devotional Twenty-Five

GOODNESS

"Surely goodness and mercy shall follow me all the
days of my life"

PSALM 23:6

The scriptures, in several Books of the Bible, offer
us many glimpses and details into the life and times
of David. He is introduced to us as a very young
shepherd boy from a large family. We see him as a
sweet psalmist, warrior, prophet and king. We read
of great victories and personal defeats and, within
the context of the whole, we are left with knowing
that the Goodness of God followed him throughout
all the days of his life.

Throughout the ages, men and women from every
country in the world have been comforted, blessed
and encouraged by the Psalms that flowed from
David's heart as he worshipped, pondered and
questioned God through all of the experiences of his
life. Such Goodness still flows today to all who read

and meditate upon these blessed Psalms. How Good and Merciful is our God.

God would also have us know that same Goodness is given to us to be a blessing to those around us as our hearts are set on following and pleasing Him. We need look no further than the life of Job, an ordinary man, who loved and walked with God. Satan tried to tell God that the only reason Job served Him was because God protected Him. He claimed that if God should just remove His protection from Job, he would curse God like every other man if Satan was allowed to test him. We all know the story of Job and the great and intense suffering he endured and how, in the midst of it all, he came forth "as gold tried in the fire." Because Job endured, his name is known all over the world today, and we are blessed by the goodness of God in the life of Job. Consider that for quite a season he sat on a pile of ashes with sores all over his body in a distant land all by himself. Lonely, to the point where even his wife told him to "curse God and die". Little did Job know he would be spoken of for thousands of years to come as an encouragement and a testimony to the goodness and mercy of God.

> "Behold, we count them happy which endure. Ye have heard of the patience of Job, and have seen the end of the Lord; that the Lord is very pitiful, and of tender mercy."

JAMES 5:11

May it be also with us that our lives may be crowned with His Goodness and Mercy. Endurance and Goodness are the offspring of Faith and are the means by which we obtain a good report unto our God. It is in knowing that His Goodness will follow us that we endure the night seasons and the lonely times, as encouraged by the scripture:

> "...let us not be weary in well doing: for in due season we shall reap, if we faint not."

GALATIANS 6:9

Let the confidence that comes from following our great Shepherd fill our hearts with the knowledge that surely goodness will follow us all the days of our life!

SELAH.

PSALM 23

Devotional Twenty-Six

MERCY

"Surely goodness and mercy shall follow me all the
days of my life"

PSALM 23:6

God's Goodness is easily seen in the life of David.
One does not have to read far into his story to
appreciate the ministrations of Mercy that followed
him throughout his days. His high points and his
low points were all entwined within the tapestry of
God's Love. His failures were followed by great
and severe judgments that even destroyed a part of
his own nation and brought reproach upon Israel
itself. However, woven into these situations was the
wonder of Mercy. There is a misconception in much
of the church today that mercy is a sentiment of
God. We are taught that Mercy is simply an
unmerited response of God to our failures and sin
that absolves us of our responsibility to walk
rightly. In reality Mercy works to make our hearts

broken and responsive to His discipline whereby we are transformed from being obstinate and stubborn to pliable in the Master's Hands.

Mercy is a power and a ministration of the Almighty God. It enables us to rise up *out* of our failures and short comings to become living sacrifices and yielded hearts.

> "I beseech you therefore, brethren, by the **mercies** of God, that ye present your bodies a living sacrifice."

ROMANS 12:1

Men and women who have received real mercy from God cannot continue to live selfish and worldly lives; for mercy captivates its recipients in a life of surrender unto Jesus the Living Christ. Mercy is the required grace to empower God's people to achieve this blessed state. Without Mercy, the best religion can produce is zealots and hypocritical expressions which mar His image in this world.

The way into the depths of mercy is found in the giving of it.

> "Blessed are the merciful: for they shall obtain mercy."

MATTHEW 5:7

Failure to extend Mercy into the lives around us

will culminate in the very springs of His life drying up within the recesses of our own hearts. A merciless life is a powerless life. A merciless life is a selfish life. Any life that has been the recipient of Mercy must become a vibrant ministration of His life.

> "Therefore seeing we have this ministry, as we have received mercy..."

2 CORINTHIANS 4:1

Mercy received produces a transformed life. The ministration of Mercy to others is a costly commodity to the giver which results in a power being communicated to the receiver. The transaction of such a precious provision is a sacred and holy one. Cheap grace and religious works will never touch the power, the dynamic and the resultant glory that emanates from these ministrations of life.

The evidence that individuals are ardently following their Shepherd will be revealed in a mercy that follows them wherever they go. The "Surely" of God is His Promise to us of such.

"Surely goodness and mercy shall follow me all the days of my life"

SELAH.

PSALM 23

Devotional Twenty-Seven

CONFIDENCE AND REST

"…and I will dwell* in the house of the LORD forever."

PSALM 23:6

The word "dwell" translated here comes from the primary root Hebrew word "to sit". It speaks of a rest and a posture of confidence and comfort. David, in his pursuit of God, came to a point where he was confident in His God, not himself. His posture of rest was not based on some teaching or the fact that he was a King; rather, his rest was based on the character of His God. This statement of confidence, **"I will dwell in the house of the Lord forever"**, had little to do with David's own ability to serve God; it was founded upon the *personal knowing* that the Lord was His Shepherd! Many of God's people struggle with this confidence, this sense of knowing and belonging. We seek for assurance by doing good things, by clinging to doctrines, assurances from others, belonging to some Christian organization, subscribing to a well-known teacher or some other outward thing to satisfy this need for security. **God has only one thing to offer us: the pledge of Himself, the verity of His own character**. Every action and motive that is not birthed from this place of abiding will eventually fail to satisfy the deep longing within the heart of His own. This place of rest cannot instill a sense of complacency or apathy. It must and will produce a pursuit and seeking of Him who has become the *One Thing* the true heart desires (Psalm 27:4, Philippians 3:13). The pursuit of Him is no longer based on gaining His approval but is birthed of an intense desire "to know Him."

> "That I may know Him, and the power of his resurrection, and the fellowship of his sufferings, being made conformable unto his death... Brethren, I count not myself to have apprehended: but this **one thing** I do... I press toward the mark for the prize of the high calling of God in Christ Jesus."

PHILIPPIANS 3:10 - 14

The one who wrote the scripture above also wrote:

> "But God, who is rich in mercy, for his great love wherewith he loved us, even when we were dead in sins,

hath quickened us together with Christ, (by grace ye are saved;) And hath raised us up together, and made us **sit** together in heavenly places in Christ Jesus."

EPHESIANS 2:4-5

The posture of sitting together with Christ in heavenly places is born of an insatiable desire to know Him more fully and deeply. It is the starting point of our journey. With this knowledge, we will arise from our failures, disappointments and trials that are all part of the discovery of both the depths and the riches of His Grace.

Trust and confidence can only be known via relationship. Such is the heart of our Great Shepherd who leads us to the "still waters" of resting in Him, the "green pastures" of feeding upon Him in the tranquility of His tender love and care, the feasting with Him in the "presence of our enemies" and to the discovery of His Presence with us in "the valley of the shadow of death"! Let us, with great humility of heart, follow Him, seek Him and grow in the graces of **The Lord Our Shepherd**!

"The Lord my pasture shall prepare,
And feed me with a shepherd's care;
His presence shall my wants supply,
And guard me with a watchful eye."

Joseph Addison (1672–1719)

*H3427. בָשַׁי *yāšab_:* A verb meaning to sit, to dwell, to inhabit, to endure, to stay. Apparently, to sit is the root idea, and other meanings are derived from this. (THE COMPLETE WORD STUDY DICTIONARY: OLD TESTAMENT Warren Baker, D.R.E. Eugene Carpenter, Ph.D.)

SELAH.

About the Author

This is Brian Troxel's first published work. He will be forever grateful for the day his Shepherd found him when he was so very lost. Since Jesus came into his life in 1974, his greatest desire has been to share His love with those who know Him and those who do not. He and his wife Linda live in Canada where they feel blessed to be close to their three grown children and their families.

Made in the USA
Las Vegas, NV
07 April 2022

47061579R00075